To See, to Build, to Win

2000—2001 NWMS READING BOOKS

RESOURCE BOOK FOR THE LEADER

CELEBRATE THE HARVEST
Edited by J. Wesley Eby

FOR THE READER

DREAMS, DOORS, AND DEGREES
The Story of Africa Nazarene University
By Theodore P. Esselstyn

IS THAT YOU, GOD?
Responses to the Mission Call
By Pat Stockett Johnston

THE MIRACLE GOES ON
European Nazarene Bible College
By Connie Griffith Patrick

THE MOUNTAIN KINGDOM
Claiming Lesotho for Christ
By Pat Stotler

TO SEE, TO BUILD, TO WIN
Volunteers for the Kingdom
By Carol Anne Eby

VENTURE OF THE HEART
Nazarene Missions in Peru
By Lela Morgan

TO SEE, TO BUILD, TO WIN

Volunteers for the Kingdom

by
Carol Anne Eby

Nazarene Publishing House
Kansas City, Missouri

To Lee,
my best friend and companion of 41 years,
who has given his entire life to others,
not only on the mission field but also
to the alien here at home.

Contents

Carol Anne Eby and her husband, Lee, were missionaries in Papua New Guinea for 20 years. Since returning from the mission field, she has been an English professor at Trevecca Nazarene University for the past 18 years. The Ebys have four children, two of which are missionaries, and 10 grandchildren. As a freelance author, Professor Eby has written for *Come Ye Apart* and the *Adult Mission Education Leader's Guide,* and she wrote the 1991-92 NWMS reading book *Wanda* about the life of Wanda Knox.

Acknowledgments

These stories never could have been written without the many shared memories and commendations given by families, coworkers, and friends. From general superintendents to grandchildren, a tapestry of love and appreciation has been woven. As the weaver, I am extremely grateful to all who so willingly took time and effort to share.

—Carol Anne Eby

Prologue

What do a Midwestern optometrist, a Southern bivocational pastor/architect, and a Canadian homemaker/teacher have in common? They have all been gifted by God for a special ministry, and all are volunteers for the Kingdom, willing to use their gifts for God's glory.

Moses waited 40 years in the wilderness before God talked to him from the burning bush. Like Moses, all three—the optometrist, the pastor/architect, and the homemaker/teacher—were middle-aged before their burning-bush experiences and before their ministry really impacted their part of the world. Yet, the result of their commitment and compassion has encircled the globe.

Paul Gamertsfelder, the optometrist, sought God's will for a new direction in ministry when an election thrust him into a unique position to lead the church in a new avenue of outreach. Don Jernigan, the pastor/architect, had an encounter with God on an airplane flying to Arizona, resulting in a million-dollar surrender. Marjorie Osborne, the homemaker/teacher, had a conversation with God from a kitchen sink that propelled her into an adventure that changed her and Canada in ways she could never have imagined. These volunteers are just normal, everyday people who have given themselves unreservedly to God, and God has blessed their efforts in remarkable ways.

As you read this book, perhaps you will hear God's voice. Your burning bush may be a kitchen sink, an office desk, or an easy chair. But all it takes is you and God for an encounter that will change your life.

Part 1

TO SEE

Paul Gamertsfelder—
A Man of Vision

Wanda and Paul Gamertsfelder

A Tribute to Dr. Paul

The church was filled, and the air vibrated with excitement. The moment had arrived. Dr. Paul was called to come forward, and the speaker began to read: "There often comes across our way someone of rare degree, / someone, who in the course of life leaves a trail to infinity. / Someone who's not afraid to go where others fear to tread, / but is willing to follow, without fail, each step where God has led." This first verse of a tribute written by Beatrice Drummond to honor Dr. Paul Gamertsfelder on the 25th anniversary of Work and Witness described a man of vision. Dr. Paul's lifework has been to help others see, not only physically but also spiritually, and to inspire Spirit-filled people to catch a vision of God's plan to redeem the world.

Dr. Paul's lifework has been to help others see, not only physically but also spiritually.

Dr. Jerry Porter, general superintendent of the Church of the Nazarene, articulated, "If the eye is the door of the soul, then Paul has seen into the soul of our missionary work. He has looked into literally thousands of eyes, prescribing corrective lenses. But at the same time, those whom he has served could see in his eyes the love of Jesus. He never complained, regardless of how long the bus trip was into remote areas. He was a cheerful, encouraging person, even when it was obvious he was weary to the bone. His love for Christ and his love for others were reflected in down-to-earth, one-on-one, practical, caring ministry to one and all."

Charles and Roma Gates recalled in 1958, when they were preparing for their first term of missionary service in Brazil, Dr. Paul examined their eyes and provided new glasses. They beautifully expressed it: "It was those glasses with which we caught our first glimpses of Brazil in Salvador with its 365 Roman Catholic churches. With those glasses, we saw where Christ the Redeemer stands high with outstretched hands over the magnificent, yet spiritually needy, city of Rio de Janeiro. These same glasses helped us see the Portuguese language in our new Portuguese Bibles and grammar textbooks. Looking through those glasses, we saw God's miraculous hand plant the Church of the Nazarene in the land of the Southern Cross."

Dr. Paul, a *remarkable* man. But his life started in a rather *unremarkable* way.

Dr. Paul's Early Life

Paul's early memories reflect both happy and sad moments. There were happy days of running around the fields and forest with his sister Mary, catching minnows and putting them into bowls as pets, and playing on their old tire swing. Paul was the third of five children and the first son, which overjoyed his father who really wanted a boy after two daughters. There were chores to be done: hoeing corn, picking bugs off the potato plants, planting peanuts in a sandy area, feeding many chickens, holding lambs' tails while his dad cut them off, skinning groundhogs, and tapping maple trees in the early spring for syrup. But the sad moments were the often absences of his father who worked on the Pennsylvania Railroad. It was depression time, and he took every job available to keep his family from suffering any deprivation. Paul remembers his mother often crying, but he did not realize the reason for her melancholy until years later.

The day had come at last: Paul was starting school. The children skipped happily along the country road that led to the one-room schoolhouse where the only teacher taught all the grades. The children gathered around the potbelly stove during cold winter days. One afternoon, they raced to the window to see the landscape filling up with snow. Blizzard conditions soon prevailed, and they were snowed in. This was much more fun than school, but at last Dad Gamertsfelder rescued them with a wooden sled. With the kids tucked under blankets, he pulled them home.

Dr. Paul's Talents and Adventures

When Paul was in the third grade, the family moved to Roscoe, Ohio. He entered a large school, which was quite a change from the one-room school he had known. In the third grade, he was introduced to music, which became a lifelong passion. His parents both loved music. His mom played the piano and electric guitar. Paul played the tonette at first. In later years, he got a French horn and excelled at that instrument, making first chair as a high school sophomore. Paul also started piano lessons as a freshman. He shared his love for music with others as a choir member and church organist, playing with his wife, Janet, who was pianist, at their local church for 33 years.

Those days of growing up at Roscoe were filled with all kinds of adventures. Paul loved to ride down the large hill just below their house on his scooter to get mail at the post office. In later years, he traded in the scooter for a bike, timing the light at the bottom of the hill to turn green so without stopping he could tear across the bridge. Climbing trees, raising rabbits, shooting sparrows with a BB gun, and climbing through culverts filled with mud, water, and sometimes "varmints" made for exciting days.

Paul had a passion for basketball but wasn't able to play as much as he liked because of family chores. But often he would slip away in the evenings and go to a basketball game at Roscoe High, sneaking in there, too, for he didn't have any money. In later years, he played in the pep band and attended all the games free. What a treat!

The zest for life Paul felt as a boy has remained through his adult years, leading him into a variety of interests: camping, golfing, boating, traveling, skiing, sailing, and flying. He has a pilot's license and a private plane, and he also owns a small sailboat. A love for photography has come in good stead as he has traveled the world.

Dr. Paul's Spiritual Legacy

Paul's spiritual legacy directed the course of

his life. Grandpa Yaw, his mother's father, would take him downtown on Saturday nights just to sit around, eat crushed peanuts, and watch the Salvation Army band play by the courthouse. Grandpa Gamertsfelder loved to sing. Piles of hymnals lay by his rocking chair, and he would often start to sing in the middle of testimony services at church. Paul sometimes sat with his dad in the choir as a young lad, not singing, but just being with him, up front, watching the people. He was proud of his dad, who was Sunday School superintendent, song leader, and active board member at Bethel Camp Meeting. Camp meeting memories include Grandma Yaw, who shouted in the aisles, and Janie Bradley, the children's worker, who led Paul to Christ when he was five years old.

Early in Paul's childhood, missions came alive to him.

That spiritual legacy and early training helped discipline Paul in his spiritual walk. Today, he arises at 5:30 every morning for an hour of devotions. He has participated in an accountability group for years, where men share together how their week has gone and how they have been a disciple and witness to family and those around them. They also share moments from their week when they have felt especially close to Christ. Jim Mason, Paul's business partner, in speaking of these times, commented, "It shows that Dr. Paul not only talks the walk but is walking it out each day of his life."

Early in Paul's childhood, missions came alive to him. He remembers missionaries coming into his home when he was only four. At the Gamertsfelder family altar, Paul's dad prayed for all his children that God would call some of them into the ministry, but this never happened. Paul was always open to a call, especially as a missionary, but at that time the church only commissioned ministers, physicians, or nurses. Paul didn't seem to fit into those categories, yet he felt God had something special. He reached 44 before he knew what that *special* ministry was to be.

Dr. Paul's Marriage and Profession

Dad Gamertsfelder wanted the best for his children and urged them to go to college and make something out of their lives. He wanted Paul to be a physician, as that was what he had wanted to be. Paul felt that profession tied down a person too much, so he opted for dentistry and regular office hours. He entered Olivet Nazarene College (now University) and studied two years in the premed program. Then Janet came into his life. She suggested optometry, which she thought was a worthy profession. Paul decided to apply for both dentistry and optometry and see which door God would open. The College of Optometry at Ohio State University (OSU) accepted him, and Paul walked through the door with no regrets—then or since.

Janet became more than an adviser to Paul.

They were married and moved into a mobile home while Paul attended school. At that time, they became active in the Shepherd Church of the Nazarene in Columbus, Ohio. Paul worked hard while in school, doing odd jobs such as mail carrier during the holiday season and baker's helper. After graduating from the College of Optometry in 1954, Dr. Paul immediately started a private practice in Columbus. Later, when the business increased, he not only acquired a larger office but also took on a partner, James W. Mason, who had been in one of the classes Dr. Paul had taught at OSU.

Paul and Janet Gamertsfelder

"I will never forget my first Saturday in Dr. Paul's office," Jim recalled. "I had just begun to work in the dispensary at the college and had probably adjusted five pair of glasses in my life. Dr. Paul had scheduled 18 people to pick up their glasses that Saturday. I thought, *Oh my, how can I ever do that!*

"Jim, just do your best," Paul responded with a smile. "I'll be here to help if you need me."

"Paul was as faithful to his 'Jerusalem' as he has been to the church around the world."

For over 20 years, Dr. Paul was there to help if he were needed, and his partner affirmed what a joy those two decades were. "A person is lucky in his life if he can count one person as his true friend and brother," Jim said. "Well, that is what I have in Dr. Paul. For 24 years he has guided me, prayed for me, and shared his life in Christ with me. I can't put into words how much I love and respect him. I know God has blessed me by letting me share in a small part of the life of Paul Gamertsfelder, and I will never be the same. I see Jesus in Paul, and because of Paul, I know that a life in Christ must be a life of service to others."

Dr. Paul found his way to Shepherd Church in 1951 after meeting Pastor Edward K. Richey at the Ohio District Nazarene campground. Mrs. Richey commented, "Paul was as faithful to his 'Jerusalem' as he has been to the church around the world." He used his musical talent, and because of his love for kids, he taught junior high boys in Sunday School and Caravan. To see progress in every part of the church, he served on the church board, the missionary council, Sunday School board, and building committee. Because he believed in outreach, he was active in visitation. When the church doors were open, Paul was there.

Paul never put personal feelings above his sense of responsibility, as proven by one memorable church board meeting. Charlene Dozier, parish nurse and then NWMS president, recalled: "Paul suddenly left the board meeting. In a few minutes, he came back and opened his palm to reveal a kidney stone he had just passed with the jaunty comment, 'The stone has rolled away!' Though evidently in pain, he felt loyalty to his responsibility to attend the board meeting."

Paul's sense of humor was often appreciated in skits, playing roles that ranged from an "absentminded professor" to "Romeo." And he was always part of the Christmas pageant, dressed in a bathrobe as one of the three kings.

Dr. Paul's Vision—Men in Missions

When Dr. Paul was setting up his practice, he was elected to the District NWMS Council and subsequently has been an elected delegate to every General NWMS Convention since. Betty Neighborgall, the chief cook on many of Paul's Work and Witness trips, said of her leader, "I really believe he actually eats, sleeps, dreams, walks, and talks missions."

In the General NWMS Convention of 1968, a memorial (motion) was made, which surprised many delegates, that two men be appointed to the General Council. This motion was voted down, as some people felt that men should come on the council by election, just as any other member.

Paul was asked to do something to get men involved in the NWMS.

The Ohio District NWMS president at the time was Mrs. Harvey Galloway, a member of the General NWMS Council from 1964 to 1972. At the 1972 Convention in Miami Beach, Florida, Mrs. Galloway placed Paul's name in nomination for the General Council. To his amazement, he was elected. Paul Gamertsfelder, along with Morris Weigelt, were the first two men ever to serve on this illustrious council.

Now, what to do with these men. Membership could always use a boost, so for Paul's first term he was appointed membership secretary. At the same time, Paul was asked to do something to get men involved in the NWMS. After going home and thinking and praying about this mandate, Paul felt it was time to get men on the mission field who had other occupations desperately needed, such as carpenters, plumbers, accountants, optometrists, and other craftsmen.

Paul called the Oriental Missionary Society office in Columbus, Indiana, to meet with Harry Burr, their director of Men for Missions. After spending one whole day "picking Burr's brains," Paul drafted guidelines of how the Church of the Nazarene could implement this program. Excitedly, he called the director of World Mission in Kansas City and told him of the vision. At first, the director seemingly did not share Paul's enthusiasm. Evidently, he felt such a program might cost our missionaries time and money. But Paul was persuasive, and the mission executive agreed to a pilot project. Dr. Paul took a small group from the Central Ohio District to Panama for a witness crusade with missionaries Elmer and Dorothy Nelson. The Nelsons were interested in going up into the mountains to see if work could be started among the Guayime (GWIE-mee) Indians and to contact the Choco (CHOH-koh) Indians in the jungle.

The following year when Paul went to Kansas City for the General NWMS Council meeting, the World Mission director had passed away, and Jerald Johnson had been elected to fill the position. After several hours of conversation with Dr. Johnson and Mary Scott, general NWMS director, and pouring out his vision to them in what he called Men in Missions (MIM), Drs. Johnson and Scott both indicated they were in favor of this movement. Dr. Johnson said, "Let's go for it!"

Since Paul had the green light, he put out directives in the *Preacher's Magazine*, *Council Tidings* (now *Mission Connection*), and other publications to promote Men in Missions in the denomination. He also used his own district, Central Ohio, as a pioneer district and organized an MIM trip to Mexico.

That first trip still stands out in Paul's memory as one of the most exciting times of his life. The all-men team left Columbus early on a Monday morning and picked up Rev. Moses Esperilla (ehs-peh-REE-yuh) in Monterey, Mexico, to be their guide and interpreter. When they arrived on the job site, a group of around 10 Mexican pastors and laypeople were ready to help the team build a simple, cement-block church with a dirt floor. Among the group was a Mexican carpenter, who was constantly followed by his three-year-old son. This man did not say anything or even appear to understand what was going on each night at the services. The team was astonished to learn this man, along with his young son, had walked eight hours from a remote village to help them even though he was not a Christian.

After 13 days on the job, the team prepared to leave the site and return to the States. Paul reported: "My van with Rev. Esperilla was the last vehicle to leave. It was just breaking dawn, drizzly and foggy. As I started to drive away from the job site, this Mexican man, with his son, pecked on my window and tried to tell me something that I couldn't understand, as he was speaking in Spanish. I motioned to Rev. Esperilla to go around and talk to him. The man told us he wanted Jesus in his heart now and asked if we could come into the church we had built and pray for him. As we knelt around the homemade altar on the dirt floor, I prayed in English and they prayed in Spanish. In about five minutes, the man came up with a big smile, shook our hands, and thanked us for being there and helping him 'find peace in his heart.' We hurried down the mountainside to find the other vehicles waiting for us, as the other team members did not know why we were delayed. They rejoiced with us. That man's conversion made the trip worth all our effort, time, and money."

Since 1973, Dr. Paul has made well over 40 Work and Witness trips.

About a year later, one of the single men who had been on that trip honeymooned in the area where the Mexican convert lived. The new groom and his bride were interested in learning what had happened to the carpenter friend. He learned, to his delight, the Mexican carpenter had gotten most of the people in his village together to give his testimony of finding Jesus. When Dr. Paul's team left, the carpenter returned to his own community and started a church, for his community had none. Stories such as this have been multiplied a thousand-fold since the Church of the Nazarene took this bold step of outreach.

Since 1973, Dr. Paul has made well over 40 Work and Witness trips to such places as Trinidad, Guyana, Nicaragua, Dominica, Barbados, Puerto

Rico, Panama, Dominican Republic, Costa Rica, Guatemala, Spain, Republic of South Africa, Kenya, Alaska, Brazil, Colombia, and Haiti. About one-third of these trips involved eye clinics, but on the others Paul was available to do anything that needed to be done.

Dr. Jim Mason, who attends a United Methodist church, teasingly said that Men in Missions might never have happened except for a Methodist. When Jim got his license to practice optometry in 1974, he had been at Dr. Paul's office two weeks. Paul said good-bye and went on a Men in Missions trip with the assurance that the "new doctor" would keep the practice going. It always made Jim feel good that Dr. Paul would trust a 24-year-old novice optometrist, who had only been in practice 14 days.

After the initial trip to Mexico, other districts started to pick up the challenge and organize trips. At that time, there was no one in the Department of World Mission to funnel trips through, so team coordinators called Dr. Paul. He would have them contact Kansas City to obtain their permission. The demand for Men in Missions' (Work and Witness) teams became so great that Rich Gammill, an employee of the World Mission Division, also devoted part of his time to this growing ministry. When Gammill left World Mission in 1979, James Hudson, a member of the division team, was asked to oversee the program along with his other duties. Missionaries Tom Pound and David Hayse coordinated team efforts in the Caribbean, Mexico, and Central and South America, where the majority of the teams were going at that time. When Work and Witness became too large for a part-time person, David Hayse was appointed the first full-time Work and Witness coordinator for the denomination.

The General NWMS Council in 1984 officially changed the title "Men in Missions" to "Work and Witness" because of the involvement of women. And the rest is history! When Work and Witness

Nina G. Gunter, general NWMS director, presenting 25th anniversary plaque to Dr. Paul in February 1999.

celebrated its 25th anniversary in 1998, the record indicated that 5,035 teams with over 88,408 participants have donated 6,027,193 labor hours or 3,093 labor years. Only heaven will reveal what truly has been accomplished.

Jerald Johnson, then director of the World Mission Division, attended the first Work and Witness conference held at the Nazarene campground in Columbus, Ohio, in 1973. It was not only a wonderful conference but a special one. Missionary Armand Doll had just been freed from prison in Mozambique. Dr. Johnson had the privilege of going into the conference and announcing that Armand had been released. It was electrifying because the entire church had been concerned and had been praying. Dr. Paul continued to coordinate the annual conference until the silver anniversary in 1998.

Over 40 mission trips render many memories. Jim Mason recounted his first trip with his partner. After working together for a few years, Paul asked Jim if he'd like to accompany him to Trinidad and learn about mission work firsthand. Jim found out what it was to be a Men in Missions rookie.

The first day on the job, Paul checked with everyone to see what type of work they'd like. When he came to Jim, Jim said, "Oh, just put me anywhere I'm needed!" That happened to be mixing cement. Paul smiled, and Jim thought it was because he was proud that Jim was so eager. Later, Jim discovered that Paul was tickled because he knew this first-timer had no idea what he was get-

Dr. Paul *(left)* with business partner Dr. Jim on the first Work and Witness trip to Haiti.

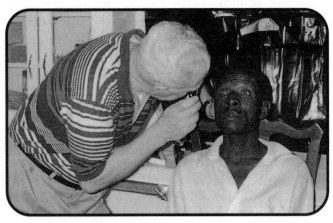

Dr. Paul still performing eye exams in Haiti in 1999

ting into. Jim thought there would be a mixer; he would just add the cement, sand, and water, and the mixer would do the rest. To his dismay, he discovered he was the mixer! He put sand on the ground, mixed in the cement, poured water into the center of the pile, and then as fast as he could shoveled the sand and cement into the water until it was mixed. For four backbreaking days, this was the routine. Then Paul announced that Jim was no longer a rookie.

Many trips followed that memorable one, especially to Haiti—16 in all. On the first trip, they sailed to La Gonave (lah goh-NAH-veh), and in three days examined and fitted 158 people with glasses. Jim recalled, "I watched Dr. Paul fit glasses on people who could not see, and what joy they and Paul received when they had sight once more. One only has to look in Dr. Paul's eyes to see Christ and his love for others."

In later years, numerous women became a vital part of Work and Witness teams. Betty Neighborgall said that Paul never made a difference between men or women's work. He willingly helped with the grocery shopping, carrying food, and sorting and distributing supplies to team members.

Another memorable trip was to Colombia. The team was riding on a bus, and Paul took out money to give for grocery shopping. Just then a big gust of wind came through the bus, taking some of the money out of the window. What a sight it was to see those by the roadside grabbing the money, thinking heaven was surely showering them with gifts!

In January 1986, Paul coordinated a large group of 39 to travel to a remote area of Guatemala. To reach this jungle site, the team traveled in an old school bus 12 hours over muddy, single-lane roads. With the luggage strapped on top, the team bounced along, hoping to reach their destination quickly. About 11 P.M. just one mile from the work site, an axle broke. The team had to unload their luggage and walk in the darkness. When they arrived, they were so tired they stretched out their sleeping bags in the run-down church and slept on the dirt floor. With that discouraging beginning and the inconveniences of such "rough" living, Paul thought no one would ever want to go back on another Work and Witness trip. To his surprise, most everyone thought it was one of the best trips ever.

Dr. Paul has influenced people not only to go but also to give.

Pastor Ken Carney from Columbus, Ohio, was one of those team members. When time came to leave, Ken shared with Paul that this trip had confirmed his call to mission service. Because Ken had four little boys at home and pastored one of the larger churches on the district, Paul honestly thought when Ken got back to the comforts of his home and loving church, he'd change his mind. But Ken's call didn't subside, and he was appointed to go to Puerto Rico to minister in an English-speaking church. After learning Spanish, Ken was mightily used in the Spanish-speaking area of the Caribbean and became Work and Witness coordinator. Who would have ever dreamed that a pastor on his first Work and Witness trip would answer God's special call and be effectively used by the Lord and the church?

Dr. Paul's Impact

Through the years, Dr. Paul has influenced people not only to go but also to give. Charles and Roma Gates shared a story about a tremendous challenge to their faith when planting a church in Brazil. They were constructing a two-story building to serve as a sanctuary and a parsonage for a Church of the Nazarene in Brasília, the nation's ultramodern capital. Funds were depleted, but by faith they were continuing the construction. Roma had made a faith promise for money to maintain a bricklayer and his helper.

Earlier in the year, the Gateses had enjoyed a visit from Roma's cousin Janet and her husband, Paul Gamertsfelder. They spent several wonderful days together. Now, many weeks later, the phone rang in the Gateses' home. After the initial greetings, Paul shocked Charles and Roma by asking, "Do you need any money down there?"

"Yes, we certainly do," Charles replied. He was about to say they needed $7,000 to enclose the new building, when the Holy Spirit urged him to increase the request to $20,000, enough to complete the construction.

Paul cheerily responded, "That is exactly the amount John wants to give!" (John Williams of Coshocton, Ohio, had asked Dr. Paul if he knew of a need for money on the mission field.) Paul was definitely used of God to answer the Gateses' prayers for funds to complete the construction. And Roma's faith promise was paid in full!

Dr. Paul has a passion to help hurting people. The Gamertsfelders' home has always been open to missionaries with special needs. Perhaps it was a shelter for a missionary suddenly called home because of a medical emergency in the family and lodging was needed while they went back and forth from the hospital. Or, as in the case of the Gates family, they needed someone to care for their teenage son while they attended a conference. Paul and Janet opened their home and hearts to an MK (missionary kid) to whom America was somewhat unknown.

Paul has suffered adversity in his own life. Jim Mason stated that one can tell the real heart of a person by his or her reaction to adversity. The day after Christmas in 1985, he was with Paul when they received the news that Janet had been killed in an auto accident on her way to visit their daughter, Adria Schumann.

Jim said: "Those next few days showed me what a man of faith Paul was. He grieved, comforted his children, Thom and Adria, and in the midst of it all thanked God for His many blessings. He did not understand why, but he trusted God and knew that His will and love were in the midst of it all. Those were some of our best-sharing days, helping me see how God was in control of his life and how all of the things that happened were to fulfill God's plan for him."

Faith held Paul in those days and until the day God brought Wanda into his life. She had lost her husband to a heart attack. Wanda and Paul were married on January 23, 1987. A new day dawned for Paul when God gave him Wanda, and together they have continued to build God's kingdom.

Dr. Paul's vision has inspired thousands to get involved in missions. When he was four, missions came alive, and he has never gotten over it. Hundreds around the world have a clearer vision today

Paul and Wanda in Haiti

because of the hundreds of glasses distributed by Dr. Paul. The bookmark he sends to those who contribute used glasses reads, "Beware! Work and Witness could be life-changing!" That has certainly been proven true in the life of this man of God—a man of vision.

Part 2

TO BUILD

Don Jernigan—
A Designer of Kingdom Blueprints

Lee Marvin and Don Jernigan

Beginning the Blueprint

The year 1925 was significant to most people as just another year of economic depression following World War I. But to the Jernigan family in Pensacola, Florida, it marked the birth of a son, J. Donald. Years later, Donald's daughter Kay Jennings reflected: "One of the things that I feel makes my dad so great is that he came from a humble beginning, and he has never forgotten it. He will still use coupons and try to get the 'best deal' on anything."

Donald's memories of those early years include the Christian influence of his home. Although his father was not a professing Christian, he instructed his children, "Be honest, tell the truth, and pay your bills!" His mother, a wonderful Christian, established the family altar where all the children gathered each evening for Bible reading and prayer. Donald's mother encouraged him as a child by playing hymns on the old piano so he could "pretend to preach." Little did Don realize then that God would call him to proclaim the gospel.

These were formative years not only for Donald and his siblings but for all Nazarenes, marked by sacrifice and commitment. Years later, Donald noted in an address to the fifth quadrennial conference on church buildings and architecture preceding the 1968 General Assembly in Kansas City: "As a young boy growing up within the Church of the Nazarene, I wondered why we had no church signs and yet suffered a persecution complex. Few people knew we existed; perhaps it was better though, for most of our buildings would not have won national awards in architecture."

Donald remembered the Pensacola Church of the Nazarene church on East Chase Street where the rent was $15 a month and the church was usually

Don, age 6, in Pensacola, Florida

six months behind in its payment. There was only one man member with just a few women and children. When Donald was about 12, the pastor, Penny Huff, visited the family. As they were eating scuppernong grapes under the arbor, the pastor said, "Don, I want you to join the church tomorrow."

"OK," the boy responded without hesitation. Don was always grateful for that decision, for he felt it helped him keep true values in focus, even during later wayward years.

Young Donald's musical expertise enabled him to play the trumpet and join the Tate High School band. Playing at high school football games was part of his fall schedule.

One day, walking to school, Don noticed an attractive young lady and asked her name. For a girl, her name was unusual—Lee Marvin Matchette. Because her father, Richard Marvin, had died before she was born, her mother memorialized him by naming her daughter Lee Marvin. Her mother also died when Lee was only six, so an aunt and uncle raised her.

Don and Lee Marvin's friendship flourished. Finally he went to her home to visit. Her guardians didn't seem too happy about the new boyfriend but allowed him to sit by her in church. Months passed. Although the young people were only 16, they were thinking of matrimony. Perhaps the times brought a sense of urgency to seize happiness. It was the early '40s, and Japan had bombed Pearl Harbor, virtually destroying the United States Navy. Don's brother J. P. convinced his parents that Don would probably have to go into the military, so they signed for their son to marry. Though Lee's guardians were not so easy to convince, they finally relented. On February 8, 1942, just after Don had reached the age of 17, the young couple was married.

Eighteen months later, their first child, Sara Kate, to be known as Kay, was born. Today, Kay declares that her mom was the solid rock behind her dad, always supporting him in his callings and ventures. "I count it such a privilege to have been raised in their home. The mother, wife, and servant of God I have become, I owe in large part to my parents."

Soon after Kay arrived, Don was inducted into the army to be stationed at Camp Blanding, Florida. Shortly after, he was transferred to a unit scheduled to go overseas—the 786th Base Depot Company. The 786th had lost their bugler, and Don was asked to take this responsibility. There was a small problem: the bugler not only left but took his bugle with him. So Don went home and brought his trumpet back to use as a bugle, which he did throughout the war in England and France. Parting from Lee to go overseas was heart-wrenching. As he held her in his arms, he promised, "Remember, if I never see you again, I will always love you."

Developing the Blueprint

After the war, the direction of Don's life took some significant turns. While in high school, he had taken manual training and drew some building plans. Since he had an interest in architecture, he decided to pursue architectural engineering in the on-the-job-training program for veterans.

Don and Lee Marvin returned to their home church in Pensacola. One Sunday night under the preaching of Aubrey Ponce, Don went forward to fully give his heart to the Lord. "That night when I went out of the church," Don said, "the stars seemed to be more brilliant than ever before!"

Two weeks later, the district superintendent, Dr. E. D. Simpson, preached in the Sunday morning service. At the close of the sermon, he came walking down the aisle and said, "Don, let's go get sanctified." With Lee Marvin at his side, they knelt at the altar, surrendering everything to God and allowing Him to fill them with His Spirit.

The trailer was so tiny Don joked, "I had to go outside to turn over in bed at night!"

In the following months, God began to deal with Don about a call to the ministry, and Don submitted to God's will. Don remembered his brother's words, "A call to preach is a call to prepare," and began to make plans to go to Trevecca Nazarene College (now University). Rev. Ponce admitted: "It was hard to give them up. Pensacola First was beginning to grow, and Don was so gifted. No matter what he was asked to do, it was always done above average."

Without looking back, the Jernigans prepared to move to Nashville. They sold their fully-paid-for house and bought a 17-foot trailer and car to pull it. They remodeled the trailer as best they could by putting an electric refrigeration unit in the small ice-box. But there was no plumbing, and water had to be carried inside in a bucket. The trailer was so tiny Don joked, "I had to go outside to turn over in bed at night!" A dinette in the front was made into a bed for their two little girls, Kay and Donna Lea, the latter arriving a year after Don's return from the war.

Nashville was a new experience for the Jernigans, especially different temperatures. Don turned on a country music program one morning and heard the announcer say, "Let's see, the temperature this morning . . . there ain't none!" He meant it stood at zero. Their trailer, partly canvas, was impossible to keep warm. Don found his shoes frozen to the floor one morning and had to pour hot water on the door to open it. But they survived, and his education began.

Dr. Homer Adams, former president of Trevecca, in writing about married students at the college commented: "Don left after classes and went to work at an architect's office, Woolwine and Harwood, where he worked as a draftsman. On weekends, he served as pastor of a home mission church. In spite of the pressure to keep the wolf from the door, he made good grades and graduated in 1951 at the head of his class with magna cum laude honors."

Trevecca made an indelible impression upon Don. Sitting in classes under godly professors, such as the A. K. Brackens and William M. Greathouse, was life-changing. Dr. Greathouse, in recalling Don's Trevecca experience, stated: "As a student in my classes, Don demonstrated a keen mind, a quest for knowledge, and above all a thirst to know Scripture and the truth of the gospel. For Don, the Bible is the primary, authoritative source of truth; any doctrine out of harmony with what he believes Scripture to teach is to be discarded and opposed."

The Madison Blueprint

Because of God's hand upon his life, Don wasn't satisfied to be just a student and hold down a secular job. He didn't want to wait until graduation to start his ministry. An opportunity opened to begin a church in Madison, Tennessee. Eager to be a part of a church plant, he met Eddie Agee, a fellow Trevecca student, in the halls one day. "Eddie, if you'll be my Sunday School superintendent, I'll pastor the church!"

This was a unique period in the history of the Church of the Nazarene. Raymond Hurn, general superintendent emeritus, noted: "When Donald Jernigan began his ministry in 1948, most Nazarene preachers were bivocational—although they had not yet used that word. Donald was busy starting a new church, obtaining an education, and establishing himself as a skilled architectural designer."

Madison was a challenge. The pioneers found a small, one-room store building. Undaunted, Don got a paintbrush, went up on the lean-to at the front, and painted "Nazarene" on the parapet. The

Home mission church at Madison, Tennessee

one room also needed to be used as the Sunday
School area. Since they couldn't afford folding par-
titions, the ladies sewed gunnysack material together and stretched a wire from the front to the
back. A creative but ineffective idea, as one could
both see and hear through the curtain. But the congregation prayed and visited until one Sunday they
had 96 in attendance. When the district superintendent heard about it, he asked, "What did you do?
Hang them on nails on the walls?"

Don Jernigan became pastor at Madison the
same year that Roy F. Smee became executive secretary of the Department of Home Missions in
Kansas City. Dr. Smee, who had been the Northern
California District superintendent, reported that in
"his" former district 80 percent of the churches

needed new buildings or improvements. He immediately wrote a booklet on financing and building churches. He also launched a concerted effort to reach out to pioneering pastors, architects, and church builders during the next 16 years. Don Jernigan would play a significant part in that effort, and his hands would be used by God to design churches not only at home but around the globe.

No cathedral ever looked any more majestic than this house of worship raised in faith, love, and tears of joy.

When the Madison congregation outgrew its facility, property for a new church was found. Don designed the blueprints under the supervision of John Harwood, the architect for whom he worked. The lot for the church was just one block from the home of Raymond and Mary Perryman. The Perrymans, who were good Methodists, had never attended a Nazarene church, but Pastor Jernigan and Eddie Agee visited them and invited them to church. The visitors enjoyed both the services and Don's ministry. Soon they became a part of the church and helped in the building program. Raymond and Don visited about 40 lumber companies to solicit framing materials. The pastor and layman didn't ask *if* they could give, but what *would* they give, and all 40 companies contributed. Even the National Casket Company gave 1,000 feet of sheathing for the roof. The Perrymans' three children and families became active Nazarenes as a direct result of their connection to Madison Church.

Don's humor helped him through some of those early building situations. The foundation of the Madison Church was so difficult to dig that sledgehammers were needed to break up the rocks. John Piper, one of the church members, was so good at the sledgehammer they nicknamed him Sledgehammer Piper. The men concluded that when God finished creating the world, He decided to dump all of the remaining rocks in Madison. Months of work followed; the building was finally completed. On the Saturday before dedication day, the committed builders sat down on the floor just after midnight and rejoiced over a "job well done." No cathedral ever looked any more majestic than

New church at Madison that Don designed

this house of worship raised in faith, love, and tears of joy.

The Inglewood and Clarksville Blueprints

The Madison Church thrived under Don's ministry. Before going to Madison, the Jernigans had attended Inglewood Church in east Nashville. When the Inglewood Church extended a call to Don, he felt it was God's will to accept.

The Inglewood experience was stabilizing for the Jernigans, and the only full-time pastorate in his distinguished career. Their daughter Kay once observed, "Daddy, you put more time into part-time assignments than most people put into full-time ones!" Their son, Donald Jr., was born while they were at Inglewood.

The Inglewood young people drafted Don to play catcher for the church softball team. His donated uniform had "Chief" on the back, so the youth affectionately called him that instead of pastor. Don confessed he could never run very fast, but he could slam the ball. One night he hit what the umpire said was the longest ball ever hit in Shelby Park!

Little did Pastor Don realize that Carlyle Apple, one of his Inglewood young people, would grow up to be a successful businessman. Later, when Carlyle made a significant gift to Trevecca, the college named a dining room in his honor, which is located in the Jernigan Student Center, built with a large gift from Dr. Jernigan himself. It would have seemed an impossible dream during those days at the Inglewood Church.

Even this early in his ministry, Don had a mission: planting churches to save souls. It was to be many years before North America was declared a mission field, but with the zeal of a missionary pioneer, Don's passion to build God's kingdom touched many lives. He was following the spirit of Phineas F. Bresee, whose mission was to get people converted and believers sanctified. As Dr. Raymond Hurn noted in his book *The Rising Tide:* "The saving of America was the 'missionary' heart cry of Bresee. He knew no difference between home and foreign fields but acknowledged 'in these days all fields are near.'"

Don prepared plans for churches all over the eastern United States. One of these church plans was for the Memorial Drive Church in Clarksville,

Clarksville, Tennessee, Church of the Nazarene

Tennessee. The congregation started the building, but just as the basement was finished, the pastor left. The district superintendent, D. K. Wachtel, asked Don to consider going to Clarksville to finish the building. Don resigned Inglewood to fill in during this emergency, but he requested Rev. Wachtel get him back into the full-time pastorate when the project was completed.

When the building was finished, the congregation became aware they owed $15,000 more than they could borrow. Don commuted to Nashville, working with Woolwine and Harwood Architects, again giving most of what he made to help pay off that debt. This was accomplished in six months.

With the emergency at Clarksville over, Don was ready to return to a full-time pastorate. However, this was not to be. The district superintendent wanted Don to plant another home mission church in Tennessee. But after talking it over with Lee Marvin, he felt led to return to Florida to start a church at Fort Walton Beach, only a few miles from Pensacola.

The Fort Walton Beach Blueprint

Don had to return to the workplace to support his family while planting a church at Fort Walton Beach. Naturally, he turned to his architecture experience. Don worked with Frank Sindelar, an architect in Pensacola. Frank was most helpful and supportive in allowing Don to do the design plans for the new church while on the job and at Sindelar's expense.

After a few months of meeting in a home, the congregation moved into a small store. Don Jr. remembers that building well. When he was about four years old, one Sunday during the sermon he had to use the rest room. He asked his sister where to go, and she pointed in the direction where it was located. Don Jr. couldn't find it, but he did find a hole in the wall, which he proceeded to explore by sticking his head though. Then he couldn't get it out! To the surprise of the congregation, and especially the pastor, a head coming through the wall was enough to stop the service for a few minutes to rescue the misfortunate toddler.

Finally, the congregation located some property and started the new building. After a full workweek, Don drove to Fort Walton Beach every Satur-

Home mission church in Fort Walton Beach, Florida

day morning, worked all day, and then returned on Sunday for the services. After the morning service, they ate their lunch, which they had brought from home since they couldn't afford to eat out. After lunch, Don rested a bit and then made a few calls before the evening service.

Don made it his prechurch chore to sit in and "pop" each pew before people arrived.

An interesting memory of Fort Walton Beach was the pews donated by Pensacola First Church. Constructed of Spanish cedar and not properly anchored together (back to seat), they would make a popping sound when one first sat down. To avoid this annoyance, Don made it his prechurch chore to sit in and "pop" each pew before people arrived. One Sunday, L. S. Oliver, then district superintendent, walked in on this strange but interesting procedure. "What are you doing, Don?" Dr. Oliver quizzically asked.

With a grin, Don replied, "Prepopping the pews!" It was a story Dr. Oliver would tell again and again.

When the first phase of the church was completed and attendance was about 70, Don felt his work was completed. Roy and Nina Fuller had just completed their ministerial studies at Trevecca, and Dr. Oliver sent the young couple to Fort Walton Beach as their first pastorate. Rev. Fuller remembers the graciousness of the Jernigans, who not only turned over the church but gave furniture to equip the parsonage. As a labor of love, Don also returned on numerous occasions to help complete the building.

The Jernigans became encouragers for the Fullers. Later, when Nina and Roy felt the call to missions, the Jernigans affirmed their faith in them by their prayers, love, and special gifts. The Fullers' call to missions also served as a bridge for Don to assist church planting in Italy. Once when Dr. Fuller returned to the States, he called Don about the need for some architectural drawings for the entrance of the church in Moncalieri (moan-kah-lee-EH-ree). Work and Witness teams could then convert a building into an inviting church. Don worked late

New church at Fort Walton Beach

into the night to prepare the drawings before Dr. Fuller's return to Rome the next day.

The love the Jernigans had for the Fort Walton Beach Church was to be rewarded in later years when Don returned to make drawings for a new sanctuary adjacent to the first unit. The church had continued to grow until attendance reached almost 200.

Later, when a district NYPS (now NYI) convention was held there, Don and Lee Marvin stayed in a motel the night before attending the convention. The next morning Lee asked, "Where are we going to eat breakfast?" Don had no answer, for he suddenly realized they had never eaten out in that area because they had been too poor. How things had changed! Don said that suddenly it seemed as if the windows of heaven opened up and God poured out His love, blessing, and grace, literally flooding his soul. It was as if God was saying, "Don, thank you for being faithful here."

Returning to Pensacola to live, the Jernigans settled back into First Church. The congregation needed a minister of music, and Don cheerfully accepted the role. Along with his architectural duties, Don became the project manager for the new control tower for the Pensacola Municipal Airport. With an improved income, the Jernigans built a nice home in nearby Gulf Breeze.

The Mississippi Blueprint

Then the call came again. A home mission church in Mississippi, Jackson Emmanuel, needed help. As before, with no regrets, the Jernigans left their spacious home to move into the back of the church that served as the parsonage. Don Jr.'s bedroom was a bunk bed in the hallway that required everyone to turn sideways and "slide by" to go to the bathroom. All of the other rooms used during the week by the pastor's family became classrooms on Sunday.

Don, of necessity, returned to his architectural work to supplement his pastor's salary. When Don showed his drawings of the airport control tower in Pensacola to the office of Overstreet, Ware, and Ware, he was hired on the spot. God's perfect timing appeared again. The firm had just entered into a joint venture with John L. Turner and Associates to do the new Jackson Municipal Airport. Mr. Turner was the secretary of the State Board of Architecture. When he observed Don's work firsthand, he told him, "You might qualify for registration as an architect on the basis of the senior examination." That required a minimum of 10 years experience in responsible work, such as a project manager. At that time, Don had 17 years experience in architectural firms. Soon a call came stating that Don qualified and had been given his architectural registration.

God's leading Don to Mississippi was certainly a landmark for future building of the Kingdom. In Jackson Don became involved in developing nursing homes. His first project after being given his architectural registration was a nursing home in Florence, Alabama. With business foresight, Don, along with several others, formed a company named Mediplex that in the next two decades would develop 50 nursing homes in five states. Don became senior vice president of the company rather than president, for he was interested in developing churches, not nursing homes. God, however, was to use this aspect of Don's life in a way that would bless thousands.

The Alabama Blueprint

When Reeford Chaney became superintendent of the Alabama District in 1964, he asked the Jernigans to consider the Mastin Lake Church in Huntsville, Alabama. The church was built, but its small size certainly stifled any opportunity for growth. The next-door parsonage was also small, especially the bedrooms. One night, Don stumbled over something in the bedroom and complained about the confined space. Lee Marvin admonished him, "Don't knock it. It's free!" With his usual creativity and flourish of his architect's pen, Don began to draw plans to alleviate the space problem.

Dr. Chaney also appointed Don the Alabama District secretary. These were good times. The church was growing, Don was becoming an active part of the district, and the family was enjoying putting down roots. But "the call" came again. Don felt God's nudge to move to the greater Birmingham area to start a new work in the area of Hoover.

When the church seemed to be thriving, Don felt again his work was completed and moved his family to Centerville, Alabama. He served as a supply pastor and later became an associate with W. E. Carruth, pastor at Tuscaloosa First Church.

Mastin Lake Church, Huntsville, Alabama

During this time, Birmingham First Church needed a pastor. Don talked to Dr. Chaney about the possibility of going full-time again in the pastorate and giving up all involvement in architectural work. To Don a full-time pastorate always seemed to be a dream just out of reach. Although he had started many churches and had drawn plans for scores more all over the country and the world, most of the time without charge, fellow pastors often asked him when he was going into the full-time ministry. Dr. Jernigan confessed that as district secretary when he brought ordinands to the altar at district assemblies, he often felt inadequate and unqualified to do so. But God was using Don's unique gifts in His own way to build the Kingdom. When Birmingham First considered someone else, Don felt

God was telling him to continue his involvement in architecture and nursing homes as a means to provide funds for Kingdom building. God was soon to confirm that to Don in a dramatic way.

The Unexpected Million-Dollar Blueprint

Don and his business partners received an offer to buy Mediplex, their nursing home company. When Don's stock was calculated, it proved to be $2.5 million—an amount that astounded him.

Don prayed silently, *Lord, if this deal goes through, help me give my alma mater, Trevecca, a million dollars!*

Later, Don flew to Phoenix where his firm had hoped to develop another nursing home. On the empty seat next to him was a publication, *Homes International*, featuring homes ranging in price from $150,000 up to $2.5 million. Suddenly the thought came to him, *If this deal to purchase Mediplex comes off, I could purchase any home in this book!* Then many questions flooded his mind—questions concerning taxes, utilities, and hired help needed. But the most persistent question was, *How could I face God someday if I took everything He blessed me with and then squandered it on myself?* Don closed the magazine, laid it down, and prayed silently, *Lord, if this deal goes through, help me give my alma mater, Trevecca, a million dollars!* End of conversation.

The business transaction didn't go through because the buyers didn't want to treat the stockholders equally. To Don that didn't seem ethical. He began divesting himself of his stock in Mediplex by transferring what he could each year to his wife and children in their family trust. Two years later, when Don actually had less stock, a firm offer to buy Mediplex came, and his remaining stock was then worth $3.5 million! One million dollars more! The Lord seemed to say: "It didn't cost you anything to honor Me, did it?" And with holy delight, Don was able to honor his commitment to Trevecca.

The Rolling Hills Blueprint

While Don was pastoring on the Alabama District, Reeford Chaney approached Don about developing a new campground nearer to the center of the district. Dr. Chaney procured about 80 acres of land for the unbelievable price of $10,000. From an aerial survey, Don developed a master plan with roadways, three lakes, and proposed buildings. Later, he designed, without charge, the blueprints for all of the buildings. The camp, now called Rolling Hills Conference Center, has become one of the nicest such facilities in the Church of the Nazarene. Dr. Chaney stated that this master plan was Don's greatest contribution to the Alabama District.

Don was elected superintendent of the new Alabama South District.

The District Superintendent Blueprint

When the Alabama District moved toward becoming two separate districts, North and South, Don as district secretary was asked to assist with the division. Several of the pastors mentioned that when the district divided they would like to see Don become one of the district superintendents. He felt it a bit unbelievable that one who was serving as a supply pastor at a home mission church would even be considered for such an assignment. But at the district assembly, Don was elected superintendent of the new Alabama South District. A bit overwhelmed, Don pledged to do his very best to God and to the people of South Alabama.

The ANBP Blueprint

Raymond Hurn emphasized that Jernigan's years as a bivocational, home mission pastor made him ideally suited to be an adviser-consultant to the Department of Home Missions, to districts, and to local churches. Dr. Hurn also believed that Don was well suited to be a leader of building professionals within the church.

From the beginning of the Association of Nazarene Building Professionals (ANBP), organized in the 1970s, Don was a key player. He was chosen as the secretary of the founding group and later served as president. The ANBP members unanimously agreed the constitution must include an international commitment to make a contribution anywhere in the world when requested. Many requests were made, and the influence of this prestigious group has reached every corner of the world. Because of Jernigan's affiliation with this group, he would be able to make an impact on the world church, reaching even to the continent of Africa.

The Higher Education Blueprint

Don always had an appreciation for higher education. But he never dreamed when the call came from his alma mater it would be the beginning of circumstances and relationships that would lead him to the most challenging project of his career. He certainly didn't realize how much he would impact higher education institutions in the Church of the Nazarene in the ensuing years.

It began at Trevecca. Mark R. Moore had just assumed his duties as Trevecca's president. In discussing the need for building remodeling at a cabinet meeting, Dr. Moore said they needed an architect to advise them. When he learned there was a Nazarene architect in Alabama by the name of Don Jernigan, Dr. Moore called him and arranged a meeting.

Don seemed just the man for the job, because Trevecca was under financial stress and the college needed a professional who understood the limitations and the professional needs of a Christian college. Don met those requirements. Because Mark

Moore had been a district superintendent, he had a deep respect and appreciation for ministers who had the vision and the willingness to make financial sacrifices to advance the Kingdom. He said that Don Jernigan knew church buildings, the pattern of people, traffic flow, building use, and aesthetic beauty. Trevecca's president found Don to have excellent taste in building style and to be adaptable, flexible, and reliable. And Don's willingness to volunteer his services was an answer to prayer. The two men often laughed together about Trevecca providing Don an office, a place to park his trailer, and no salary! Dr. Moore could not and would not forget Don Jernigan.

Another Nazarene institution of higher learning had a special need. Don was invited to visit Nazarene Bible College in Colorado Springs. He was there at the invitation of Jerry Lambert, president at the time, whose job was to design a chapel and conference center in memory of the founding president, Dr. Charles Strickland. Don made many trips to Colorado. He listened for endless hours to the board's dreams, plans, and wishes, successfully capturing their ideas and weaving them together with his own years of experience as an architect, builder, pastor, superintendent, and church leader. The end product of the Charles Strickland Memorial Chapel and Conference Center has been such a success and tribute that Hiram Sanders, current president of the college, said, "It's a perfect building and more than adequately fits every purpose of its original design."

The Africa Nazarene University Blueprint

Another call came that took Don's expertise from his "Jerusalem" of the South and his "Samaria" of the rest of the United States to the "uttermost parts of the earth." It had been a dream in the hearts and minds of missionaries and church leaders for years. It was born out of the desperate need for highly qualified African Nazarenes to lead in the roles required of them. When missionary Harmon Schmelzenbach went to Kenya, he was overwhelmed by the dozens of young people who wished to become part of the ministry of the Church of the Nazarene. At last Richard Zanner, Africa Regional director, presented to the field directors and Ted Esselstyn the possibility of a seminary to be located in East Africa.

Nearly a year passed in the search for adequate land. Dr. Schmelzenbach and his wife traveled 13 miles south of the bustling city of Nairobi, home of some 2 million people. Leaving skyscrapers behind, they stepped onto wild, untamed African grassland covered with thornbush and rocky soil. The plot overlooked a deep gorge with water running far below. Wild animals roamed the land. But as Dr. Harmon gazed at the peaceful hills turning purple in the setting sun, he claimed the land for God and the church. African Nazarene University was about to emerge from dream to reality. The land had been owned by four different African tribes, but God was in it. The transaction for the land, together with the change of user permits, all went through. The pieces of God's plan began coming together.

Mark Moore was appointed to establish the graduate seminary. The land was available, but the land needed buildings. And when Dr. Moore thought of buildings, he thought of Don Jernigan. In late 1987, Dr. Moore called Don and asked if he would be interested in going with him to Kenya to help in the planning of the proposed seminary. There was nothing Don would like better, so he met Mark Moore in New York in early 1988 to fly to Nairobi to meet Harmon Schmelzenbach and Ted Esselstyn. The men lived, talked, worked, and dreamed together for one week as they tried to envision what would be needed.

Don was honored with the dedication of the Jernigan Chapel at ANU.

As a result of that meeting, Don prepared a master plan for the entire site, including preliminary plans for the dormitories and chapel. The first building was to be a chapel, making a statement that the church would remain the center. It was thought at this time that the institution would be a seminary, but soon it was discovered that a graduate seminary could not issue degrees unless it was part of a university structure that issued undergraduate degrees. From then on, everyone started talking about Africa Nazarene University (ANU). Don took the news in stride and, along with other members of the Association of Nazarene Building Professionals, prepared drawings for the initial buildings. In addition, Don designed a stone and ornamental iron gate and fence on the front of the property with a high chain-link fence on the other three sides to enclose about a quarter of the property.

Dormitories at ANU, part of Don Jernigan's master plan

Countless Work and Witness teams over the next six years constructed buildings, and a beautiful university came into being—debt-free. During those years, Don made six more trips to Africa at his own expense, sometimes with his wife and other members of the family, always deeply concerned that his vision of the campus would materialize. Because of Don's contributions, which were in excess of $100,000, today impressive buildings of hand-cut stones, steel rafters, steel reinforced concrete floors and pilings, covered with clay tile roofs should last for many decades. He donated literally thousands of hours and shared fully in his heart the vision that was held for the training of young people in Africa. In September 1993, Don was honored with the dedication of the Jernigan Chapel at ANU.

As Don Jernigan looks back over his 70-plus years, one of the guiding principles of his life has been to "invest your life in those things that outlast it." If you would visit over 200 churches he has designed, or the Rolling Hills Camp in Alabama, or the campuses of Trevecca Nazarene University, Nazarene Bible College, and African Nazarene University, I believe you would agree with him that truly he has lived by those words.

TO WIN

Marjorie Osborne—
A Woman Called of God

Marjorie Osborne

Marjorie—an "Un-ordinary" Woman

"You're nuts, you're nuts! You'll get a knife in your guts!"

The chant reverberated through the neighborhood from the lips of a street person glaring at Marjorie as she stepped from the car into Eastside Vancouver, British Columbia. Dr. Charles Muxworthy, then district superintendent, and his wife, Dorothea, were bringing Marjorie Osborne to see the site of Mission Possible, a compassionate ministry located there. What a welcome to downtown Eastside! More timid souls might have been scared off forever, but not Marjorie. Undaunted, she continued her visit, and the incident brought many laughs as the story was told again and again.

Marjorie Osborne is not an ordinary woman because of her sense of optimism and adventure. Those who know her well describe her as cheerful

Mission Possible in Vancouver

and upbeat with a keen mind, able to assess situations and people quickly. K. C. Macmillan, pastor of Moncton First Church in New Brunswick, said: "Marjorie lives and breathes evangelism! She draws energy for evangelism from a deep and confident relationship with God; she expends that energy by being creatively engaged with lost people wherever she encounters them."

Marjorie seems to be equally at home discussing her faith with her Jewish financial adviser, her Muslim real estate agent, or a homeless, destitute drug addict at the Yonge (YUHNG) Street Mission in Toronto. Marjorie's love for urban life and people is gripping. She is a contented urbanite, apparently reveling in the complexities and contradictions of city living.

Marjorie lives and breathes evangelism!

For many years, the Church of the Nazarene seemed hesitant to engage in urban ministry. But the denomination in recent years has targeted large cities for evangelism and church planting. In 1990 the Thrust to the Cities focused on Toronto, and God had been readying His servant Marjorie to lead the thrust.

One of Marjorie's greatest assets is grim determination. She will not believe a door is closed until every last effort has been exhausted. Her brother, George, commented: "God took a young lady with a pretty good temper and changed her completely. He didn't take the fire out but rechanneled it for His glory."

Marjorie—a Loving Relative

Doors slammed and people spilled out over the front yard. Another family gathering was taking place, and Marjorie basked in the warm congeniality of her family. Aunts, uncles, cousins, and—best of all—Grandma were there to eat together, laugh a lot, and enjoy each other. Marjorie's father's parents had been killed in a car-train accident when he was 16, so all of his brothers and sisters were orphans. Her mother's dad died before Marjorie was born, so there was only Grandma, who lived to her late 90s. Little Marjorie became closely attached to her and visited her almost every week.

In Marjorie's growing up years, World War II ravaged Europe. And though items like gasoline and sugar were in short supply, the war seemed far away. Marjorie and her brother saw uncles, aunts, and parents of their friends go to war. Some didn't come back, but the closeness of the family and the warm fellowship shared through the years seemed to shield the children from the horrors of war. Although all of the family weren't Christians, several gave their lives to full-time Christian work. One cousin is serving today in Venezuela with New Tribes Mission and another at radio station HCJB in Quito, Ecuador. Family reunions are still a great event, although they happen less frequently as the family is spread all over the world.

Marjorie—a Child of God

Marjorie's memories of childhood were most positive, but her religious roots were quite complex. Her father was a lay preacher in a little mission that held services in a lodge hall. Preaching was about being born again, although the children really didn't understand that at first. Hymns were sung from a red-covered hymnbook, Sankey's *Sacred Songs and Solos*. Because of a shortage of gas, the family went to church on the streetcar. When this group disbanded, Marjorie and George began attending Sunday School at the local United Church of Canada. Eventually they found themselves in a Baptist mission. During her teen years there, Marjorie was involved in singing duets, playing the piano, and taking part in young peoples' meetings.

"The breeze was so fresh and clean. God had changed me."

When Marjorie was 13 years old, she won a prize in Sunday School to go to teen camp. Even though she had been in church all of her life, she had no idea of what being a Christian really meant. Free spirited and a bit rebellious, she had to adjust to the rules. It was hard for her to give up playing cards under the sheets. Sitting through those classes and evening services, however, placed her under deep conviction.

One afternoon, she ran away to the woods,

knelt down by a big rock, and began talking to God. She confessed her sins, and He graciously took her burden away. The encounter was so exhilarating that many years later she said: "I can still feel how that rock felt under the sun, firm and warm. The breeze was so fresh and clean. God had changed me." Struggles were not over, however. She often thought she'd wear the rug out in front of the altar at the church, but God was molding her into submission.

Marjorie—a Happy Nazarene and Bride

When Marjorie was 18, she met Ed Osborne. She was still a part of the Baptist church, and Ed was in the Main Street Church of the Nazarene. Marjorie's church had a wiener roast at Scarborough Bluffs, a picturesque part of the Lake Ontario shoreline in Toronto. Both Marjorie and Ed had other dates, but she was impressed with this young man's ability to get along well with people. Ed must have been impressed, too, for he came to the Baptist church the next Sunday afternoon for Sunday School and invited Marjorie to the evening service at the Nazarene church. She went after a warning from her father that if the congregation did anything strange like "fainting or swinging on the drapes," she should leave immediately! Marjorie found the people lively but quite sane.

A few months later, she and her brother, George, moved into the Nazarene church. The denomination was new to them, but the preaching of entire sanctification was something that drew them, something they needed in their own lives. The pastor was enthusiastic, and the congregation loved them. In 1956, Marjorie and George joined Main

Ed and Marjorie Osborne at wedding reception

Street Church and knew they had found a place of worship that was right for them. Eventually their parents joined too, and Marjorie's dad attends that same church today.

Marjorie thought Ed was wonderful. Some of their first dates involved cutting grass in a field, helping erect a tent, and attending the meeting (Marjorie was pianist) that was held to get the Kennedy Road Church of the Nazarene started. More dates followed. The couple's friendship and courtship led to their I-will-love-you-till-death-parts-us vows on December 20, 1958.

When Marjorie graduated from high school at 15, she wanted to be a nurse. But when the nursing school wouldn't take her until she was 18, she decided to become a teacher. She graduated from Toronto Teacher's College at 16 and began teaching kindergarten. Rounding out her skills, through summer and evening courses, she became a primary specialist. She worked for the Toronto school board for eight years.

After Marjorie was married and teaching school, she finally submitted her life totally to God. That encounter renewed her vision; she thought the sky had never looked so blue. She went downtown and—all of a sudden—she felt an overwhelming love for the people she passed. She *really* saw them, and realized she loved them for Jesus' sake.

Marjorie—the Devoted Homemaker

Although clearly capable for the workforce, Marjorie chose to stay home and devote herself to the care and development of her two sons, Andrew and Michael, and her husband, Ed. She was not interested in pursuing a career or higher degrees, but she did find ways to acquire the knowledge she needed. As her schedule permitted, she studied English, Italian, and psychology at the University of Toronto, urban missions at Tyndale Seminary, and creative writing at Seneca College in Toronto.

Marjorie's home is an active, busy place. She always has an endless list of stimulating things for her family to do. Yet, the Osbornes' home is simple. Accumulation of wealth has never been a signifi-

Marjorie and Ed with their son Andrew and his wife, Vivian

Son Michael and his wife, Karyn

cant value; joy and delight are found in the simple things of life and in close communion with the Lord. Not that they couldn't have enjoyed more luxury, but they deliberately chose to live in Christian simplicity. Ed is a mechanic with Honda and has worked for the same dealership for over 40 years. He is very good at what he does, and his income has always allowed Marjorie to work for the church as a one-dollar-a-year staff member.

To her children, Marjorie is an exceptional mom. They say the qualities that make her so exceptional are wisdom, patience, unselfishness, optimism, and common sense, all wrapped in a spirit of love for God and family. They enthusiastically applaud her sense of adventure.

Marjorie—the Intrepid Adventurer

When the Osborne boys were almost teen-agers, Marjorie planned an expedition to the jungles of Venezuela. There she was at her best, sleeping under a canopy of stars while her "men" kept the fires burning and the scorpions away. When she heard that raiders might be on the way, she still went to sleep, relishing in the adventure.

One year she planned a trip to the Arctic Ocean. The family traveled the Alaskan, Klondike, and Dempster highways. Arriving at Inuvik (ih-NOO-vihk), they were still short of their distance by 250 kilometers (155 miles). After Marjorie found a plane and a pilot, they flew to Tuk (TUHK). Cutting a hole through 18 inches of ice, they stuck their toes in the Arctic Ocean, which had been Marjorie's goal.

Canoe trips and camping excursions are Marjorie's favorite "torture," according to her family, which often take them to new and inaccessible places. After two weeks in the wilderness, Marjorie is in her element. They set up camp in some lakeside spot, remote and picturesque. Then, they stay put for days, learning to tell time by the visit of wolves to their beach at 6:30 A.M. or a moose passing their camp at 8:45 A.M. as it slowly makes its way up the water's edge.

No matter the difficulties of wilderness living, Marjorie is undaunted and always ready for the next adventure. Ed laughingly says, "To Marj, heaven is a shoreline. When she arrives in heaven and is shown her mansion on a street of gold, she'll ask to be downgraded to a tent with a silver river running by." However, Ed admits that her visionary and adventurous spirit throughout the years has honed her for the work she now does for the kingdom of God.

Marjorie—the Obedient Servant

Marjorie's work was not identified quickly. At age 36, she read *Jungle Pilot*, the life of Nate Saint, martyred missionary to Ecuador. In chapter 16, Nate reflected over his call to be a missionary. He wondered if he had wasted his life by preparing for another career, but then he realized everything he had prepared for, God was using in his new vocation.

> ## "There's going to be a change in your life," God whispered.

Marjorie often wondered if the Lord had something special for her to do, and in conversation with Him, she felt divine affirmation. But what? She had been teaching piano lessons to neighborhood children. Maybe it was a musical career. Later she took a writing course and found that she loved it. She had some stories published and wondered if this was God's intent.

One day, a decade later at age 47 while Marjorie had her hands in the kitchen sink, the Lord spoke to her. As she looked out the window with the autumn sun of a gorgeous September day shining on the brown shingles of the roof next door, the sun rays were almost like the rays of fire from a burning bush. "There's going to be a change in your life," God whispered.

Change? Marjorie felt like Sarah laughing after the angel's announcement of Abraham's expected heir. Nothing ever changed in Marjorie's life. She had been married over 26 years. Her husband had worked at the same job for 29 years. For many years she and her brother had lived only five houses apart. She had been in the same church for almost three decades. *Change?* What an absurd thought!

In the next few months, nothing seemed to change, but still Marjorie felt a deep assurance God was going to do a new thing. In April, with her hands in the same sink, and now a bright spring sun shining, the Lord spoke again, "You're going to change churches."

Marjorie's response was, "Lord, how are they going to do without me?" She was a Sunday School teacher and the church pianist. She and Ed sponsored the young people of the church, and they loved those teens. (One of those youth, Deryl Price, is today a Nazarene missionary in Nigeria.) Marjorie was active on the district on the Sunday School board and NYPS (now NYI) Council. Dr. Bill Stewart, her pastor for 11 years and now national director for the Church of the Nazarene Canada, commented on the deep Christian commitment both she and Ed exhibited in the local church.

God's answer was, "The whole world can get along without you, but they can't get along without Me." Marjorie had her commission to go and win others.

Shortly after, Marjorie went to Anaheim, California, as a delegate to the 1985 General Assembly. Sitting in the meetings, she sensed the Lord saying over and over, "Ten thousand Canadian Nazarenes are not enough." During the Sunday morning service at the baseball stadium, she promised the Lord she would give the rest of her life to change that number, if He would show her how.

As soon as Marjorie returned home to Toronto after General Assembly, she received two significant telephone calls. One was a pastor inviting her to become the church planting director for Rosewood Church—the daughter church of her home church, Main Street—to plant two new baby churches. The Rosewood pastor remarked that his church had started talking about the project the previous September, and she had come to their minds as one to lead the endeavor—the exact time God told her there would be a change in her life. As mentioned before, Marjorie saw the beginning of the Kennedy Road Church in a tent meeting, and this evolved into a church that later planted Altona Road Church in Pickering, Ontario. Being involved in land searches for these new churches made a deep impression in her heart for church growth and church planting.

The other phone call was from her doctor. "You have a large tumor on one of your kidneys," he told her, "and you need immediate surgery." The removal of a kidney would seem to be a deterrent to anyone's dream, but Marjorie's fierce determination came through. Soon she was up and about, busily carrying out the plans God had given.

Marjorie—the Toronto Thrust Coordinator

A year later, Marjorie was asked to head a committee to formulate the Toronto proposal. When Toronto was designated the Thrust City for 1990, she was appointed to see the proposal through to completion as the coordinator. At the same time, she was elected to the district advisory board and the Canadian executive board. She believed the Lord had taken seriously her commitment to the Church of the Nazarene in Canada. Knowing God had called her to be a "missionary" in her own county, she was amazed at how He was fulfilling that call.

> When God gives a dream,
> He gives a big one.

In working out the proposal for Toronto, she called 14 pastors to bring their most visionary leaders to a meeting. They were all men. Since this had to be a cooperative effort, Marjorie knew it would be a tremendous job—if not impossible—to get all of these men to work together. But after hours of labor, they developed a 24-page booklet.

The next day, three of the pastors called Marjorie and thanked her for her leadership, saying how good it was to have a woman lead them. They assured her that a man would never have gotten them all to agree. That experience made up for the time she spoke at a gathering of U.S. district superintendents. When she entered the room, one gentleman asked her if she had brought the coffee, not realizing she was the speaker of the evening.

When God gives a dream, He gives a big one. Toronto was an ideal choice for an evangelism thrust. Although Canada stretches 8,000 kilometers (almost 5,000 miles) from the Atlantic to the Pacific, 60 percent of Canadians live within 800 kilometers (about 500 miles) of Toronto. Toronto not only has the population concentration but also is the financial and cultural hub of the country. But, more than that, Toronto is a multicultural city; thousands of immigrants and refugees move to Toronto each year. Only 47 percent of the population is Anglo. The other 53 percent represent more than 100 different languages. Many people in Canada still consider the Church of the Nazarene a cult, and most of the 4.6 million people of Toronto are unaware of the presence of the Church of the Nazarene.

In spite of the need, great challenges stood in the way. Land in downtown Toronto, if any became available, was priced at $20 million an acre. Modest three-bedroom bungalows sold for $400,000 and rented for around $1,500 a month. Rent for one service each Sunday in a school gym cost between $600 and $900 a month.

Though the problems were many, the proposal targeted the planting of 27 new churches, 10 among new language groups. The proposal set out to operate four Christian counseling centers in needy neighborhoods; coordinate Christian day-care for children in Nazarene churches; and establish a government-sponsored, church-operated seniors' residence and seniors' day-care assistance programs. In addition, the proposal provided for equipping and training people for Target Toronto ministries; appointing Target Toronto committees to carry out the proposal; soliciting support for Target Toronto by raising $1 million and enlisting 2,000 people to pray daily; and making full use of all denominational resources; and participating in Vision 2000, a plan put together by Canadian evangelicals.

The ambitious proposal was accepted. Marjorie, as coordinator, knew it could not succeed unless there were miracles. She had no idea where the personnel and finances would come from, but she was in partnership with a big God.

Some of the best miracles have been people. A young Chinese pastor with an American wife stepped out in faith to plant a Chinese church. With no congregation, he started house-to-house visitation. The first door he knocked on was answered by an Anglo, but the man was friendly. He said they were moving, but a Chinese family was moving in the next week. When the pastor returned, he found not only a new house owner but an old friend, his Christian high school teacher in Hong Kong. He and his wife and three children were overjoyed to become part of the new congregation. And he knew another Chinese, who became the first convert of the new church.

Marjorie—the Dynamic Visionary

A church in downtown Toronto that in the 1950s had been a vibrant congregation of some 350 had dwindled to 20. The pastor just wanted out of the situation. Relocating him cleared the way for two visionary college students to come, and they transformed the old church into a center for refugees called "The Sharing Place." They had enthusiasm, vision, and energy, but no money.

That year at district assembly, Marjorie had a God-inspired idea. She bought a heavy chain with 180 links. Whenever someone gave a donation of a hundred dollars, she would cut off a link. She took her chain to district assembly and laid it down by the piano. When called to make her presentation, she picked up the chain and put it around her neck. She took only a few steps when she knew this was a mistake. The chain was so heavy that wearing it for 10 minutes was going to be agonizing. One of the pastors joked, "You'd think Marj has been buying her junk jewelry at K-Mart!" She felt weird but began to talk about the lonely and homeless of Toronto.

Marjorie had only spoken a few minutes when a pastor got up and said, "Marj has carried this burden long enough." When she sat down, people started to come forward and drop $100 bills in her lap. A pastor went out and brought back chain cutters. In 20 minutes, she had $18,000 instead of the heavy chain. A soloist sang "Little Is Much When God Is in It," and God came in a wonderful way. Dr. Jerald Johnson, presiding general superintendent, chose not to preach and led the congregation in a time of celebration, saying, "Don't look around the world to see where God is at work, because He is at work right here and right now."

Marjorie thought, *This could be the most hopeless person I've ever met.*

It was at The Sharing Place, made possible by that offering, where Marjorie experienced a special revelation of God's work. One day, while sitting at a table interviewing people coming into the center, she saw a man with a cane approaching. He looked

The money raised for The Sharing Place

sick. He had no winter coat, no pillow, no blanket; his eyes were filled with hopelessness. Marjorie looked at him and thought, *This could be the most hopeless person I've ever met.* In talking to him, she felt led to say, "Have you ever had anything to do with Sunday School or church?"

"Strange you should ask me that," the man, named Jim, replied. "I was a clergyman, but don't ask me where God is, because I haven't the faintest idea!"

Marjorie, taken aback, didn't know how to react. "Would you like to tell me how that happened?"

Jim poured out a story that broke her heart. Pointing to a lovely church near the center, he said: "I used to pastor there, but I had two children who died of cancer before they were two. My wife said, 'I'm not going to serve a God that let that happen!'"

As the man related his story, Marjorie learned that Jim's wife left him. Bitter and broken, he turned to alcohol and lost his family, church, friends, and health. He became a cab driver, but because of his drinking habit was unable to keep that job. The streets became his home.

"Jim, would it be all right if I pray with you?" Marjorie asked. He agreed, and she prayed that God would send hope into his heart. He had no glasses, yet his eyesight was so poor, he couldn't see well enough to pick out some clothes and food to take home. Marjorie loaned him her glasses and then took him to the place where he was staying. That evening, Marjorie told her family about the most hopeless man she had ever met.

Several months later, Marjorie and Ed met a pastor from South Africa who had run away from a rebellion and immigrated to Toronto. He needed a winter coat, so the Osbornes took him to The Sharing Place. When they entered the center, Marjorie noticed a sharp-looking volunteer at the interview table. During the evening, the man spoke to Marjorie: "Do you remember me? Do you remember I said I don't know where God is? Well, He answered seven prayers for me this week!"

It was Jim. Happy and gainfully employed, a new light shone in his eyes. "Do you want to know what made the difference for me?" he asked. "You loaned me your eyeglasses and gave me a ride home." Tiny acts of compassion. But just enough to turn Jim's life around.

At every step God brought just the right person along. One of these was Marjorie Serio (SEE-ree-oh), the lady who now administers Some Place Special and a person called on to set up other centers across Canada. She came to Marjorie Osborne one day and said, "I believe God woke me up last night to talk to me about Christian day care." Mrs. Osborne says she has proven to be a gem. When God calls, He calls the best person for the job.

Ian Fitzpatrick, a pastor, spoke to Marjorie one night after a Target Toronto meeting. "The Lord just keeps on saying to me, 'Target Toronto, Ian. Target Toronto!' Marj, if there's a particular place you need me, I'm ready." After praying several months, Marjorie felt Ian should be the church extension director for Target Toronto. He was exactly the right person, and God knew he would be.

Marjorie had no idea where the pastors would come from for the new language congregations, but the Lord brought an Egyptian, a Portuguese, a Filipino, a Hispanic, and a Chinese. In an interview with Michael R. Estep, then director of Thrust to the Cities, in the spring 1990 issue of *Grow* magazine, Marjorie declared, "The Lord adds people to vision for sure—people to lead, and now as the new works have started, people to be saved and become part of the church!"

In the beginning of the Toronto Thrust, many miracles provided finances. Not only was the money for the compassionate center raised in 20 minutes at the district assembly, but an automotive company donated $22,000 of new winter clothes. Marjorie had no idea how they knew about the project. A lady in a town an hour away from Toronto called to say she had 25 new quilts ready. A Work and Witness leader said, "We have $5,000. What would you like us to do?" Many other Work and Witness teams followed. One team from Oklahoma put 53 gallons of paint on an old downtown church, built a new pastor's study, and renovated nursery and toddler rooms.

Since 1990, God has continued to speak in the missionary thrust in Canada. One night in a service in Winnipeg, a young lady sang "I'll Be a Servant." During the song, the Lord spoke to Marjorie, "Are we still doing the job? Are we still working on this country together?"

Marjorie responded in awe, "You really meant it, Lord. You are putting me in a place where I can influence the whole country!"

The record proves it. Before 1988, all metropolitan churches were likely to be in suburbia or in the city, dying. But now the churches reach many different kinds of people. They do not all have buildings, but they worship in sundry ways and support a variety of ministries. Before 1988, worship was conducted in English, French, or Armenian, but now 14 other languages are heard in some 40 churches that are non-Anglo or French. In 1988, compassionate ministries were nonexistent, but there are now 11 major centers in seven cities. In 1988, laypeople didn't have a great desire to work outside the church nor were they particularly encouraged to do so. Presently the Church of the Nazarene in Canada has launched the Commission on the Laity that is bringing and will continue to bring vast changes. In 1988, there was consternation because the Toronto Lay Training Institute was launched, followed soon by the Toronto Nazarene Bible Institute. At a recent meeting of the National Board, it was decided that all five districts in Canada would have this type of ministry development centers by the year 2002. People are dreaming citywide dreams in Halifax, Toronto, Calgary, Winnipeg, Vancouver, and Edmonton. There's been a genuine acceptance of the urban missionary concept and a freedom to work at it all across the country.

Marjorie—God's Servant

Today, Marjorie is away from home about 120 days a year. Her present position is church growth coordinator for the Church of the Nazarene in Canada. She reports to the national director quarterly and to the National Board annually, and she keeps each district superintendent informed of con-

On cross-country tour of Canada's districts in 1988. *(Back, l. to r.)* Curt Harrison, technician; Marjorie and Ed Osborne. *(Front, l. to r.)* Paul Skiles, then Communications Division director, and his wife, Maxine; Alice and Jerald Johnson, then general superintendent.

current activities on his district. At national, district, zone, and local levels and, in keeping with the "national vision," her duties are to communicate vision for evangelism, church planting, church expansion, and compassion evangelism. In addition, Marjorie's responsibilities are many and varied: assisting with the strategy and implementation of church growth projects; seeking to elevate prayer in relation to evangelism; motivating and coaching lay involvement in Kingdom-building ministries; offering seminars and workshops in urban mission, church planting, church growth, and evangelism; facilitating a network for the purposes of encouragement and exchange of information; and researching and circulating church growth information within the Church of the Nazarene and other denominations.

Marjorie has recently given much attention to Mission Canada, the Canadian arm of the North American Urban Mission Process under the auspices of Tom Nees, director of Mission Strategy for the U.S.A. and Canada. She has been a part of the development of this initiative from its inception and has endeavored to explain, promote, and implement the process with the districts. Eventually, career missionaries will be assigned to work with the districts in major population centers, but along with this there is the need to continue to develop comprehensive urban strategies. Marjorie strongly believes that while career missionaries will be extremely valuable, what could be accomplished might be short-circuited if the urban missionaries, both lay and clergy, who are already hard at work are overlooked. She has taken and will continue to take every opportunity to help the Church of the Nazarene impact the 25 major cities of Canada.

As an indication of Marjorie's busy schedule, in 1998 she presented 32 seminars on such topics as "Sharing Your Faith," "Vital Church Growth Principles," "Churches in Transition," and "Planning for the Future." Besides the seminars, her speaking schedule included 25 worship services, 5 college/seminary chapels, 4 urban conferences, 6 other denominational assemblies, 2 television shows, and 2 radio broadcasts.

The Osborne children are now grown and away from home, yet Marjorie wondered what her husband's reaction would be to this new direction of her life and her hectic pace. "Are you going to be all right with this or just grin and bear it?" she asked him. "Or, are you going to be in it with me—lock, stock, and barrel?"

Marjorie has felt the mantle of Isaiah 61 fall upon her.

Ed looked at her and said, "You're not the girl I married. And none of this was in the original contract." But God had been preparing Ed's heart as well, and he has given his full blessing to Marjorie's ministry. In December 1998, they celebrated their 40th wedding anniversary. Their children gave them matching bikes with automatic gearshifts, so they anxiously awaited the snow's disappearance to begin a new adventure.

Ed says Marjorie is a driven woman. He laughingly remarks that if the world were like him, horses would still be used for transportation and coal oil for light. But not Marjorie! If she were in charge, we would be living in some quadrant of outer space or on the ocean floor.

Marjorie with her grandchildren: Lindi, Brook, and Kaitlyn

Marjorie Osborne is no ordinary woman but a woman called of God. She has felt the mantle of Isaiah 61, her favorite Bible passage, fall upon her. And with God's Spirit, she wants to change her world.

Despite a full life as wife, mother, homemaker, local church member, and national church growth coordinator, she has made time in her busy schedule to look after grandchildren on a part-time basis until they become school age. Her daughter-in-law Vivian sincerely believes only God himself knows the extent to which her children's lives have been enriched by the quality time they have shared with their loving grandmother. Vivian recalls, "I was listening to my six-year-old son, Brook, say his prayers, and among other things he prayed, 'And God, please help Grandma to do her job well.' I know that this prayer has already been answered. Whether in her role as church worker or grandmother, she has done her job well."